Growing upAmish

Insider Secrets

from One Woman's

Inspirational Journey

Anna Dee Olson

Creative Genius

An Imprint of Morgan James Publishing • NEW YORK

Growing up Amish

Library of Congress Control Number 2007935665

ISBN: 978-1-60037-334-3 (Paperback)
ISBN: 978-1-60037-335-0 (Hardcover)

Habitat for Humanity®
Peninsula
Building Partner

Published by:

MORGAN · JAMES
THE ENTREPRENEURIAL PUBLISHER™
www.morganjamespublishing.com

Morgan James Publishing, LLC
1225 Franklin Ave Ste 32
Garden City, NY 11530-1693
Toll Free 800-485-4943
www.MorganJamesPublishing.com

Cover/Interior Design by:
Rachel Campbell
rachel@r2cdesign.com

Edited by: Ronda Del Boccio
Ronda@AwakenTheAuthorWithin.com

Read & Edited by:
Nancy A. Ruskowsky
Cody, WY

Contact the author at: http://www.GrowingUpAmish.com
Email: anna@GrowingUpAmish.com

Within the pages of this book is an unprecedented look at the major events of one woman's journey while growing up Amish. Although there were many happy moments, that lifestyle also proved to present many challenges. GROWING UP AMISH *gives you a look behind the curtain. You will learn how the author has become a stronger person because of her experiences to live the healthy, happy, and love filled life she lives today.*

Testimonials

The information Anna Dee presented on the Amish was from personal experience and was both informative and inspiring.

The question answer time was an important part of her presentation. It was obvious listeners felt free to ask any question and Anna Dee was forthright in her answers that lead to more questions.

This topic was of special interest to our community because we have so many Amish families in our community. However, I believe it is of interest to any community to better understand those who are different from us. There is also more interest in the Amish people after the school teacher and girls were murdered and their response to this tragic event.

Marilyn Breckenridge
Pastor- Wadena, MN

I THOUGHT IT WAS VERY informative. It showed how what an amazing life they live. Unless a person has lived that way of life, you don't know why they live the way they do. It reminds me of someone being poor and not knowing how the richer people live.

Yes, we always see the Amish going past our home and in the businesses and you often wonder what their lives are about. After hearing Ann's story, I can see that they take their culture very serious.

I feel since there are so many Amish spread across the country and in so many communities, that it is good for the general public to know how their lives are lived.

I think that speaking in schools and churches would be a good place to get a mixed group of the general public. There could also be community meetings set up by town leaders. In fact if they had a community meeting with coffee furnished and maybe juice and people would come and then maybe shop in the town afterward. So it would benefit the community as well.

MARIE FRAUNE
Wadena, MN

MY HUSBAND AND I WERE at a presentation that Anna Dee gave about the life of the Amish people. Previously all we knew is what we had seen on television and heard about the Amish people in our local area.

What we have learned from Anna Dee helps us to understand why they live the way they do. The questions she encouraged people to ask after her presentation were very interesting and informative.

I know there is a lot more to know and I am looking forward to reading your book.

DEE SCHWARTZ
Wadena MN

A CAPTIVATING STORY OF REAL life in the Amish Community and how the determination of a young woman who knew that life outside the walls of the Community would be a better life - one she was going to have no matter how hard the struggles would be.

This book is a gripping account of reality too harsh to bare, yet a fascinating look at the culture and an easy read. I couldn't put the book down until finishing it and am looking forward to her next book.

JOAN SOSALLA
Whitehall, Wisconsin

DEDICATION

I DEDICATE THIS BOOK TO my mother, 74, and my father, 73, whom I love dearly. I thank you both for sharing with me the values of simplicity, hard work, and the graciousness of our Lord and Savior Jesus Christ. I have derived so much pleasure and benefit from this and I am particularly grateful for having the chance to grow up in a larger family and for all the joys we shared together as a family. Without you Mom, Dad I would not be who I am today.

I also dedicate this book to my wonderful husband whom I love so very much. You are the person I dreamed about as a very young child. You support me unconditionally, without judgment, and only provide the best for me. I love you.

My last dedication is to my son and daughter whom I also love so very much. Both of you have been the quiet inspiration behind keeping me going with my book and my passion to help others. You are so much more to me than I ever dreamed life could provide me. You complete my circle of love.

ACKNOWLEDGMENTS

FIRST OF ALL I WANT to say thank you to my husband Tom. Part of God's plan for my life was to meet you. You give me unconditional love and support. You are my rock, my inspiration, and my soft place to fall. If it weren't for all your help, understanding, and encouragement this book would not have been possible. Thank you to my son Joshua and daughter Jasmyn. You two bring me so much love. God new I needed you to complete my circle of love on a daily basis. I could not imagine my life without you.

Secondly, I was to say thank you to all of my new found family and friends. Especially my mother-in-law and father-in-law, Joanne and Marlin, my good friends Penny, Jon, Kailee, Jonathan, and Tricia, Joan, Cathy, Bonnie, Edna and all my other friends, too numerous to list. Thank you all for being a part of my life.

Next, I want to thank my mother and father, all my siblings, and everyone in the community where I grew up. Life was not always easy but through faith and prayer I now totally understand that you all did the best you knew how. With deep gratitude I say thank you for being a part of my life. I whole heartedly forgive you all. Even though sometimes there were sad and hurtful moments, we also had lots of happy times. Every moment that I spent with each and everyone of you helped me to become the person I am today. For that I am very thankful to have met and got to know you.

   With Gratitude

Anna Dee Olson
www.GrowingUpAmish.com

TABLE OF CONTENTS

Chapter 3

Chapter 4

Chapter 5

FOREWORD

IN THE TIME THAT I have known Anna, one thing has become very clear: her deep commitment to learning, growing, and being the best she can be in all that she does. In this book, *Insider Secrets of Growing up Amish*, Anna is inspiring and empowering others to follow her lead to be the best they can be!

Anna came into our (my husband, 3 children and I) lives in 1991, after she left a timid but friendly message on our answering machine, in response to our ad in the classifieds looking for a baby sitter in our home. We jumped on the opportunity to have someone stay at our house to help care for our children. Anna was a 23 years-old-adult when we went to meet her at her parent's place. Still I think she did a lot of growing up after we met

Her journey before and after leaving the Amish culture has me in awe to this day. *Insider Secrets of Growing up Amish* provides a detailed depiction of Anna's early years. You may get the feeling that parts of her journey was rather simple but don't let her fool you. She worked very hard and she had to overcome many obstacles and emotional feelings to move forward. Even though there were many bumps in the road for Anna, her determination was big enough to always find a way to keep moving onward and upward. As you read through various chapters of Anna's young life; you will see that she shares tools that she was able to believe in, found helpful, and even healing, after years of struggling.

What Anna reveals in *Insider Secrets of Growing up Amish* is deeply personal and I am touched to have known her for sixteen plus years and to have played a role in her journey. For Anna to share at this level is so opposite from how she was taught so I am amazed at the growth that she has gone through. Anna was a young adult when we first met and I couldn't be more proud if she were my own child. She is an incredible adult…with a great family and career to be proud of.

Now to top it all off, she is willing to share her own experiences and/or mistakes to help others. I enjoyed *Insider Secrets of Growing up Amish* entirely! When I started reading I couldn't stop until I got to the end of the book. I am looking forward to her next book for more details about her unbelievable journey. Anna has so much for you to learn from so I would suggest you get your hands on everything that Anna allows you.

PENNY PAULSON
B.S. Psychology
Case Worker
Franciscan Skemp Healthcare
Arcadia, WI

Preface

Insider Secrets of Growing up Amish

*One woman's inspirational journey away from
and back to Amish culture.*

Where did Anna Dee Olson come from?

Anna was born in Jefferson City Missouri in 1968. She was named after a family friend who was also her mother's Maud (helper/maid) at the time. From a family of ten children, Anna was baby number five. Anna has five sisters; two older and three younger and four brothers; two older and two younger than herself.

Her parents were married near Bowling Green, Missouri in April of 1962. They lived on a small hobby farm and her father ran his own sawmill. The first baby came shortly after the first year of marriage so then her mother was busy taking care of the child, cooking, cleaning, gardening and canning food, and sewing all the clothes. With each child the family grew and so did the workload.

Anna and her family lived in Missouri for eight years and then in October 1969 they moved to Wisconsin to an 80 acre farm. Anna's parents did some farming, plus her father continued to operate the saw mill. The family moved into small but typical story-book cottage type of home with oak trees, lilac bushes and flower beds all around. The house was setting in a valley with a hill to the east and north; the driveway wound over the hills and through the woods to the west, and to the south it was all downhill perfect terrain for sledding.

There were three bedrooms; two upstairs with an open stairway and a master bedroom on the main floor. There was a fair-sized living room where we had a wood stove as our main heat source. The kitchen/dining room was all one room. We had a wood cook stove in the kitchen, which also helped to heat the house. The basement was dark and dingy, but it was a good place to store our canned goods, potatoes, and other vegetables harvested from our garden each year.

After four years, Anna's father wanted to move to Minnesota. So in October of 1973 the family moved to northwestern Minnesota onto a 28 acre hobby farm. Anna's father continued to operate a custom sawmill for an income. To keep the children busy Anna's parents grew and harvested cucumbers for the local pickle factory a couple of years. Other years they raised strawberries to sell. Anna's family always had a big garden and lots of produce to preserve for eating during the winter months.

In February of 1984 Anna's family moved back to Wisconsin due to the dwindling Amish in their community. Anna's parents wanted to live in a community where there were more young folks (Amish people not married yet) so Anna and her siblings had more choices for life partners. Anna's parents still live there today.

After Anna left the Amish culture in 1992 she started college classes in LaCrosse Wisconsin but then moved to northwestern Minnesota to finish the first two years of college at Minnesota State Community and Technical College. Anna graduated with a Diploma in Word Processing with a Computer Emphasis in 1995.

In 2005 Anna graduated from Minnesota State Community and Technical College for the second time with an Associate Degree in Medical Secretary. Anna's main passion for leaving the Amish culture was to attend college. Anna is very proud of that accomplishment.

Anna is sharing her story in this book in hopes to be an inspiration for others to change and improve their own life. Anna had many obstacles to overcome to live the happy life filled with love and respect she lives today.

Anna is no better than anyone else, so if she can do it you can do it. Anna had a dream for her life. She did not realize it, but God had a plan for her too. Because Anna never lost track of her dream of a better way of life, she is now able to live that lifestyle. Growing up Amish was not easy; Anna was not allowed to express herself in many ways which prevented her from learning the essential life lessons to survive.

As you read this book, pay close attention to how each event affected Anna at the time, how she overcame the event, and what she learned from the experiences. Anna truly believes that each experience; as hard as it seemed at the time; occurred so that she could become better person.

This was God's plan for her life. When Anna decided that she did not have to be Amish to find salvation, immediately her life began to change for the better. She just needed to pray for help and guidance. Again if she can do it you can too.

This is the first book that Anna has written and she is very excited to say that there will be more books to come. Anna has an amazing story of how low she sometimes got in life and how she changed her habits to change her life.

Do you want to hear more from Anna? Visit www. GrowingUpAmish.com and enter your name and email address in the form on the homepage. Come along with Anna and she will share many valuable scenarios' and tips to better your life. How can this shy Amish girl (not knowing anything about the outside world) even think of leaving the sheltered community behind? How does Anna survive and create a healthy and happy lifestyle full of love and respect that she lives today?

What was/is God's plan for your life?

CHAPTER ONE

The Power *of* Persuasion within an American Culture

Growing up Amish, the Myths vs. Reality

Anna, age 22, dressed casually

Growing Up Amish

Growing up Amish proved to be quite a challenge for me. Now that is not the case for everyone. This is my story and I write from the heart and from what I know to be true, no myths or outside observations included.

A couple of things I want to share with my readers before you read the pages of this book.

My parents did the best job they knew how. Raising a family of ten children is not easy as I am sure anyone would agree. My mother did not always agree with my father when disciplining my siblings and me, but they did their best to not let us know there was a disagreement. If my parents argued they waited until all the children were in bed or they went to the bedroom and closed the door.

Amish folks do not attend parenting classes, nor do they believe in reading books to get parenting tips. Amish parents take pride in the fact that they are carrying on the family traditions just as their parents did. Tradition is a great value.

The children are taught to be obedient, no questions asked. My job was to do as I was told without argument or explanation.

Growing up Amish meant that we lived simply; we did not have electricity, television or radio, vehicles, or indoor plumbing. At the time I felt that we must be better than the outside world because we don't have all these sinful things in our home. However, my parents did not feel that way. My mother always said that we are not here to judge anyone else. We can only take of our own.

We only used hand-powered tools in the kitchen or the shop. The only news we received was through the uses of snail mail or newspapers. Our transportation was horse and buggy. If we wanted to travel farther than we could go with horse and buggy we would hire a non-Amish person to take us in their vehicle. And our bathroom was a small outhouse behind the house, to be used both summer and winter. We took baths by carrying the water heated on the wood stove to a galvanized tub in the living room next to the wood stove.

We did our laundry with the old wringer Maytag washer run by a gas engine that was mounted to the machine. Very noisy..... We did our yard work and gardening with hand tools. The grass on the lawn was cut with a manual push mower.

This lifestyle is simple but not easy. As you read the pages of this book you will learn that some of the obstacles I had to overcome were uncalled for and not right. Every family has secret issues they have to deal with and everyone is different. However, I truly believe that all of my obstacles played a huge role in developing the person I am today. Hard work built character in me and today I am not afraid of a challenge.

I chose to not be a product of my upbringing. By that I mean that a couple of years ago I decided that my childhood problems will no longer define who I am today. I made the decision to leave my family behind to search for a better way of life. Now I am not suggesting that everyone has to go to that extreme, but it was the only choice I had at the time.

With much determination, faith in myself, and small steps of action every day I am able to experience a happy life today. My hope is as you read this book you will see how doom and gloom my life was at times but not always. We had many happy moments and I cherish those memories very much. But also I hope you can realize that I am no different than anyone else. If I can use simple steps to change my thought process to change my life then it is also possible for you.

Thank you for joining me in this journey. Enjoy the book and remember I do have more books in my brain to be coming out soon! Keep watching my website for update information.

CHAPTER TWO

How *a* New Discovery Made *a* Plain Girl Beautiful

How do you look at your body image?

Anna (right) and her sister (left) in everyday dress

Does Extra Body Weight Define You

Let's not forget that the little emotions are the great captains of our lives and we obey them without realizing it.

-Vincent Van Gogh, 1889

It was easier to eat more food than to deal with the emotions inside. Fat, ugly, and disgusting were just a few of my feelings.

Why was my father telling me I was fat enough? Does that mean he likes me or hates me? At first I had no idea, but by the time I was three years old I understood that fat was not a good thing.

Being called fat is the ultimate way of demeaning another human being. Every time I heard another remark about my weight it felt as if someone had put a knife through my heart.

Why does a person of bigger size need a label? When we call someone fat; are we trying to make ourselves feel better about our own weight? Because of my experiences I now make a conscious effort to see people for who they really are and not their appearance. There is a deeper self in everyone. We just need to look for it.

While visiting my sister and her family I observed her daughter being ridiculed for her weight. My heart was bleeding of pain for her. Although I was not able to voice my thoughts; I did write a letter to let my sister know how those comments affected me and potentially could affect her daughter. I truly don't want to see anyone else have to experience the effects of demeaning comments about their weight.

This is what I discovered from my life experiences. The realization was huge for me. I wished I had known about this many years ago so I would have been able to see life in a completely different way.

If someone comments about your weight it simply means that they are not happy with their own weight. They are only trying to make themselves feel better. For whatever reason, they feel the need to bring your attention to what they are thinking of themselves.

When I discovered this I was not longer around the key people that constantly reminded me of my weight. But it was so interesting how I changed as a person, from no self esteem to having all the self confidence needed, when I changed my thinking process.

Try this the next time you get a comment that sound like an attack on you, "I am so sorry, how can I help?" It may astonish the other person but then explain why you said that and mostly like you will not hear another comment like that from the same person.

Were You a Child Who Just Wanted To Be Understood

How does a toddler learn the meaning of fat?

Should a toddler know the meaning of fat?

As I grew up Amish I was considered to be fat, not overweight or obese, but simply fat. I learned this unfortunate fact when I was three years old. One might ask how this pertains to a three year old. I will share some instances where I was told I am fat which will help you understand how and why.

We did not have visitors very often but once in a while my aunt (that lived in our community) or one of the cousins would come to spend the day. At first I thought it was great to have visitors but then I began to associate being called fat with any time the cousins visited our home.

I had no idea what that meant but they would say to me, "I am not going to play with you anymore because you are too fat". Or they would say, "I don't like you because you are too fat." I was too young to understand what was going on. I just assumed they said those horrible things to me because they hated me or wanted to hurt me. It made me feel very sad and unwanted.

It did not take me very long to figure out what fat meant. Within a year or so I began to realize what was really going on. My father helped me understand what fat meant. Our family always gathered at the table for breakfast, lunch and dinner.

One evening as we were eating dinner I requested a second helping of food when my father said to me, "you don't need more food, you are fat enough". The only thing I understood was that I am not getting any more food and he hated me for asking.

After hearing comments with the word FAT included a couple of times I began to realize that I was different than the rest of my siblings. I stood in front of a mirror and studied my body. Why was I bigger in size than some siblings older than me? Why was this happening to me?

My father may have been correct about me not needing more food but I will never forget how hurtful those words were to me. My interpretation of the FAT comments was that I was disliked because I was FAT. Why does my father hate me? What did I do that makes him hate me so much?

Today I know he did not hate me but was using it as a teasing tool. I am sure he had realized how it was affecting me he would not have continued to use my weight against me. At three years old that is all I understood and it took me many years before I was able to sort it all out.

So remember this as you think about your own struggles as a child. Was it really as bad as it seemed? Isn't it amazing how our minds work sometimes? This is really where my struggles with myself, my parents and siblings began.

Did You Want To Lose Weight Before Six Years Old

O ne afternoon during the winter my mother had set up the little round bathtub in the living room next to the warm stove to give us all a bath. While I was in the bathtub I remember looking at my stomach and wishing I could just take a knife and cut it off. Maybe then my father would not have to constantly remind me how FAT I am.

Now remember I was only three or four years old when all this was happening. How could I make it stop? I wanted to please my parents so much but it did not matter what I did, I was reminded of how fat I was all the time.

Every child does wish to receive approval from the parents? I wanted my father's approval with every thread of my being. I just wanted them to recognize me for who I was and not what I understood from the horrible words I was hearing. I was also compared to someone else all the time, either one of my siblings or someone in the community.

This really was the point where I began to constantly compare myself to others and eventually I did not really exist anymore. I had no idea who I was or why I was born into this world. All my energy was put into trying to be like someone else. That is the danger of being compared to others as a young child.

The point here is that I was only three years old and already aware of my appearance. Can you imagine the amount of guilt and worry this alone put on my shoulders?

Today I know that my parents loved me. They grew up without affection so they did not know how to give and show love to my siblings and me. With the knowledge and training I have today it is hard for me to imagine how a mother cannot show love for her children by giving them a hug no matter what age they are.

But I also know what it is like to live in a state of tradition. I did not miss my mother giving me hugs because I did not know what that was like. My parent's role was to provide food and clothing for me, teach me right from wrong, and make sure I followed the rules of the community.

If only they knew to love us unconditionally; skinny or fat or anything in between.

Because of my experiences my awareness is so much clearer. My children will not have to wonder if I love them. I will not allow them to compare themselves with others. By God's gracious love for us he created us all to be unique. Who are we to try to change that in someone's mind?

Are You Different Than Others.....Why Do You Think So

Very quickly my brothers and sisters figured out that it was acceptable to call me fat. Whenever it was convenient for them they called me fat. "You can't have any because you are too fat." "You can't play this game because you are too fat." Many times I complained to my mother that I was called fat yet again. Her answer to me was always the same, "Awe Anna, you know they are just teasing you to see if you get mad. Don't let it bother you and they won't say it again." I really don't think my mother thought there was anything wrong with calling me fat. I heard the fat comments from my mother too but not as often as from my father, siblings, and school mates.

At the age of twelve years old I knew I weight had skyrocketed to over one hundred pounds but I refused to step on the scale. I truly did not want to know how much I weighed. However, my brothers (one older and two younger) would not give up on wanting to know.

Visually they could see I weighed more than my older brother but that was not good enough; they wanted proof. They set up my father's old-type hospital scale in the shop; asked me to come in the shop and then forced me on the scale. It took all three of my brothers to force me to stay on the scale, but eventually I got so tired that I gave in and let them get a number. After they let me go they weighed themselves and subtracted the difference.

I felt so embarrassed. This was a direct violation of my privacy. In the process of trying to keep me on the scale my dress was torn. My mother was very upset with me when she saw the tear.

After all that they discovered that I weighed one hundred twenty seven pounds. During dinner that evening my brothers were so proud to tell my parents how they tricked me into getting on the scale. "Can you believe Anna weighs one hundred twenty seven pounds already?" I don't remember my fathers' exact words but he did get a good chuckle from this whole ordeal.

It was never fun for me to be the center of attention when it was about my weight. I did talk to my mother privately after supper that evening. I wanted her to understand how violated if felt and I am sure she knew but her answer to me was the same as always;

"Awe Anna they are just trying to tease you. If you don't care what they say then it won't be so much fun to try again."

Today I can understand my mother's point of view and she was right; it is part of human nature. However, because of this experience I can also feel the victim's side and I will never let this type of teasing occur in my children's life. Young developing minds do not need to bare this burden.

Suffice to say, I never stepped on that scale again.

Did You Know Prayer Can Be Very Powerful

One day I saw my mother praying to God for things she wanted in her life so I decided to pray to God that I would not be fat anymore.

In my mind my prayers were never answered so as I got older I asked God to show me why I deserved this. Again I did not get the answers I was looking for.

Our prayers were always done as a family. After breakfast in the morning we all gathered in the living room, knelt on the floor next to your chair while my father read a prayer out of the prayer book. The prayer book was in High German which made it very hard for me to understand what we were praying for. We also bowed our heads for silent prayer before each meal and also after each meal. After I knew the Lord's Prayer I recited that in my mind during meal prayer.

Since prayer did not seem to do the trick for me I turned to food for comfort. It was easier for me to eat more food than to deal with the emotions I felt. Food became my comfort; food did not call me fat; food did not tell me how much it hated me; food did not tell me I couldn't; and food would not tell me I could not play. Eating more than I needed was my way of dealing with the trauma that I was dealing with.

As a teenager I was very desperate to find some kind of control of my eating habits and my weight. Eating too much only worsened the situation so I did the opposite. I skipped meals as much as I could. However, this only caused me to gain more weight because when I did eat I ate enough to make up for the meals I missed.

Our diet consisted of protein, starch, and sugars; mostly starch and sugars. At noon we ate the biggest meal of the day and the main part of the meal was potatoes. Mashed potatoes were the family favorite. When my mother decided what food to make for a meal she would first determine how to prepare the potatoes and then what else to go with that.

Most of the time supper consisted of some kind of soup and crackers with fried potatoes or canned meat. We did not eat lettuce salads, baked potatoes, steaks, or any grilled meats.

For breakfast we usually had hot cooked cereal with fried eggs and bread. Sometimes I would make biscuits and tomato gravy with fried potatoes. We also ate pancakes, French toast, and once in a while cold cereal.

The fruits and vegetables that we did eat were mostly canned. In the summer time we had lots of fresh garden vegetables. This was pretty much the only time we ate lettuce, but not in a salad format. We ate lettuce sandwiches. We also ate radishes, kohlrabi, green onions, peas, bean, and corn. During the summer our diets were so much healthier than in the winter time.

Keep reading for more details on how we preserved our foods.

Is God In Control In Your Life, Or Who

Yes, I grew up Amish but that does not make me any different than any other child. Hearing a snide comment once in a while throughout your life; a person might say this is bearable. But how can an innocent child defend themselves when it is almost a daily occurrence?

God was watching over me throughout all this and he knew I needed to have some challenging experiences so that I would become a better person. There is good in everything; if only we can see it. It took me many years to see the good in this but now I also know how to look for it.

Only God would know but I may not be able to help others today if I had not endured all this. For that I say thank you God for showing me the way.

Sometimes I wished my life would end so that I would not have to hear another snide FAT comment. I dealt with those feelings by finding a happy thought. I spent many hours voicing my perfect life to myself. I would imagine that I was perfect size and the only people in my life really wanted to know me for who I was. Yes these thoughts were my fantasy land but it really helped me to cope when I did not think I had any other place to go for help.

As traumatic as this experience was for me I feel I have learned so much from it. Fat comments are not a part of my life or my relationship with my children today. This experience was traumatic enough to stick with me for many more years but I never lost site of a better way of life someday.

Now as I reflect back on these experiences I realize how naive I was. I did not know that I had to learn to love myself before I could expect anyone else to love me. In counseling years later I was taught that I needed to love me first. That was a challenge for me but it is so true and it feels wonderful.

After I left the Amish culture I learned that I needed to love me for being me and no one else. How did I change my thoughts and habits? This was not easy but it was important. Everyday I looked at myself in the mirror and said these words out loud, "God has created this person and he did a beautiful job." "Who am I to belittle that?"

If you are having a bad day just remember that you are a creation of God. Someone cares if you live or die. I forced myself to use positive self talk. Yes some days it felt very uncomfortable to do that but I had a dream.

Focus was my number one survival tool. People were able to distinguish my self esteem and self worth but they could not take away my dream. I had a dream to live a better life. You could say my tunnel of focus was very narrow and I did not let anything stop me.

Many days were filled with doubts and I would learn later that is very common. It just means you are right on track. If you feel like the challenge before you is too much, just remember what your dream/goal is. I know sometimes I took a day or so to feel sorry for myself and regroup but then I was right back on track. Be patient and change one habit at a time. Experts tell us it takes twenty one days to establish new or rid your self of old habits. Also make sure to celebrate your success as they happen.

Would You Like To Be A Fly On The Wall

The general public believes that most Amish children are so well behaved and you never see them acting out. This is true when they are in public but please remember that they are no different than any other children. Amish children do misbehave and are mean to each other sometimes.

In American culture today it is not cool to call children fat or ugly, particularly not adults. In the Amish culture it is viewed to be okay to use snide comments to demean others. I truly don't believe that my parents saw it a problem to use fat to describe me. I heard many adults from my community, including my parent, describing others with words that are not very nice.

Yes, I was taught to be respectful to others and name calling was unacceptable. But then I would hear my parents call me names. You can see how confusing that was for a child.

I don't think my parents realized that they were not very good role models for what they were trying to teach my siblings and me. So I grew up thinking the rule is simple: "Don't do as I do, do as I say".

If you are wondering if I was able to ever work my way through the stigma of my obesity. Yes I did and now I will give you some step by step process I used to do that.

I had quite a lot of built up anger so to start the process I wrote out all my thoughts. If you find yourself having angry thoughts about someone or something; take a pen and paper and write it all out. Write exactly what you are thinking and don't leave anything out.

The best part about this process is that you don't have to care what you say because nobody but you will read it, or that is what I did. Even though I shredded my writings I still felt much better afterwards.

Also, remember to treat your mind and body with kindness. Tell yourself you are just what God wanted you to be and it does not matter what any earthly person says. The reason I hated being called fat was because I believed it. In my heart I truly looked at my body as fat and disgusting.

To change this self talk I took time everyday to look in the mirror and say something nice about what I saw. Yes there were many times I wanted to let those old tapes in my brain play again, but I got out of bed the next day and said something nice again. After a while I was reminded of those nasty thoughts less and less. And today I only remember when I choose to do so.

The moment I stopped believing the FAT snide comments, I was able to begin the healing process. I separated the wonderful current side of my life from my past. Don't dwell in the past for you cannot change it anyway.

Live for the moment and focus on the future. Look for something wonderful every day.

Cooking/Baking The Amish Way

Cooking for a family of twelve people, three meals a day was an art on its own. We had to figure out what to cook for each meal. Sometimes my mother would ask what we should make for the next meal before we had finished the dishes from the current meal.

My mother taught me to cook and bake when I was six years old. I loved to bake and sometimes I would end up with a cake not fit to be eaten but that is how I learned. One time I wanted to make homemade grape nuts. The recipe asked for either brown sugar or molasses. Well I did not read the directions well enough so I put both the sugar and molasses in the dough. Let's just say we had some very sweet grape nuts.

Another time while stirring up a chocolate cake batter I forgot the baking powder. The cake did bake but did not rise so it looked like brownies but believe me it did not taste like brownies.

Other things that I learned how to bake were; breads, cookies, all kinds of cakes, pies, sweet rolls, and donuts. We always had home-made bread on hand which meant we would make six loaves of bread every five days or so.

I loved Saturday's because it meant that I could spend all morning baking pies. Since I enjoyed baking I would choose that duty over cleaning. My sisters were happy because they would rather clean than bake. Sometimes I would bake anywhere from eight to twelve pies on a weekly basis.

My memories of baking in that small kitchen with yellow painted walls and a green/yellow checkered floor; on the old wood burning cook stove are a real treasure to me. The smells from the fresh baked goods were to die for. It felt very rewarding to know that I had spent hours creating something that everyone in my family loved.

I was taught to not feel proud of myself or anything I had done but at times I could not help it. Particularly when I tried a new recipe and it turned out to be delicious.

It was tradition at our house to make raised donuts every year at deer hunting season. On opening day everyone got up at 3:00 AM to get all the chores done and by 6:00 AM when the guys left for hunting.

As soon as the men were out of the house we stirred up the dough (which included mashed potatoes) and it would have to set for an hour to rise then we could roll it out and start cutting donuts. Again the dough would rise for about forty five minutes and then it was ready to deep fry. Last we would apply a sugar glaze and the donuts are ready to eat. Yum...Yum.... This was all done by 10:00 am when the hunters returned for a break.

I really enjoyed cooking and baking. It was my way of creating something that my family could enjoy. Sometimes I was ridiculed for my cooking, especially when the food did not turn out just right. But I also received many compliments. Those were the happy moments which I treasure.

There was a saying among the Amish people that when a young girl can roll out perfect round pie dough and it fits the pan just right, then she is ready to get married. I tried it thousands of times but I don't think I ever got it perfect. But it did help me to try my best.

Most every Amish girl dreams to get married, have children, and become the best mother and wife you can be. That was my only goal for the first 18 years of life.

CHAPTER THREE

The Best Kept Secrets *on* Childhood Discipline

Is obedience the only choice?

Anna and her nephew

Who Is In Charge In Your Home

If there is anything that we wish to change in the child,
we should first examine it and see whether it is not
something that could better be changed in ourselves.

~C.G. Jung, Integration of the Personality, 1939

Some of the discipline I received I felt was very unnecessary. It was just a way for my parents to relieve their frustrations by inflicting pain upon the children. Why not just explain to me what I did wrong and why it was wrong?

I reacted with frustration and anger, which brought on more discipline without explanation or a hug to let me know that it would be okay in the end.

When my mother told me she had to spank me because she loved me, I did not understand. How can you inflict pain onto someone you love? Quite simply it taught me at a very young age that hitting, kicking, and pinching are the way to relieve my frustrations.

If only my parents could have sat down with me and talked about what I did wrong and why it was wrong. I longed for that connection however, I never was granted that privilege. My parents refuse to discuss any of these things with me, even today. I am quite sure it is because they don't know how to provide that kind of support. They did now grow up that way and so I have accepted the fact and moved on.

I don't discipline my children in the same fashion. I love my children and I could never inflict that kind of pain to them. I want my children to know that I will love them no matter what they have done. They can always come to me with anything and everything. There is a better way.

My father was very concerned about having enough money to keep food on the table for ten children. My mother was busy taking care of the children and sewing to keep us in clothes. I think that was their first priority. So what I am saying here is learning how to be an effective disciplinarian was not a priority for them. They disciplined us exactly how they had been taught while growing up and that is how they expected us to carry the tradition forward.

The Secrets of Effective Discipline

Today in American culture it can be very challenging to discipline your children in the appropriate manner. It seems to me that each culture has its own appropriate and inappropriate rules about discipline.

Do you discipline your children in the same manner as your parents disciplined you? Although I was disciplined the Amish culture way and now of course I discipline my children the American culture way or at least for the most part.

The difference that I see here is simple. In Amish culture spanking, hitting, and pinching (and even worse forms like pulling all of a child's teeth for punishment. See the story at <u>www.amishdeception.com</u>) is an accepted way of discipline. In American culture this is not okay. Yes, I know it does happen but I also know parents have had their children taken away by Social Services because of this kind of abuse.

I don't discipline my children without physical abuse because it is not accepted in American culture but rather that is not what I believe to be acceptable. Parenting does not mean you have the right to harm anyone. It means you have the responsibility to teach and nourish your children to adulthood.

Secondly, the fact that I do it differently than my parents is the generational difference. Things change over the years; trends come and go. Discipline is the same way; what was appropriate in American culture years ago is no longer acceptable today. I know my children have given me some very challenging moments. What I wanted to tell you about in this section is how I was disciplined at home; how I felt about that discipline at the time; and what I learned from the experience.

My parents believed that children should be seen and not heard and they also believed in spanking, if necessary. By the time I was one year old my parents started to teach me that concept. I was expected to sit in church for three to four hours and not make a sound, or as little as absolutely possible. I was allowed potty breaks, and up until I was eight years old, we were given a snack to eat and water to drink midway through the church service. Once I turned eight years old, they told me I was too old to have a snack.

At home I had a bit more freedom to be child-like, but again I was spanked with a belt quite often. Nothing was explained to me as to why I needed to be spanked. When I was a little older and started to ask questions, I asked my mom why she had to spank me. The only answer I ever got was, "because I love you." That did not make any sense to me. How can you love me and then spank me so hard that you leave red marks on my skin.

As I reflect back on what happened and how I felt about it at the time, I realize why I was spanked so many times. As a child I needed their attention and this was the only way to get it. Think about that in your own children's behavior. If only my parents could have taken the time to sit down with me and explain to me how I was supposed to act and why. But that did not happen so don't miss doing that with your own children.

There motto was to spank the child and send them to bed or off to do another chore. I know I was not a "bad child" and certainly not any worse than any of my siblings. I found a way to get some kind of attention, even if it meant another spanking, it was better than none at all.

Mostly I got spankings for not getting my chores done in time or acting out when I felt I was being picked on. The other forms of discipline my parents used were pinching my earlobes, hitting me on the shoulder and whipping with a willow whip.

These forms of discipline left me feeling very unwanted, unappreciated, and certainly not a child of love. I was not being heard by anyone. Even my mother was not willing to hear my side of the situation nor was she willing to talk about it later.

My experiences can be a great lesson for others. If you find yourself screaming and hollering at your children too much of the time, stop and think about it. Are they looking for attention? Do they need your love and understanding? And most of all make sure you explain to the child why their actions were inappropriate and what your form of discipline will teach them. Children are very smart and will understand much more than we give them credit.

When I was nineteen years old I was asked to help with chores at a cousin's home while some of their family had traveled to another state for a funeral. On the Saturday forenoon my little sister and I had gone to town to get some groceries that we needed. My father was not happy that we gone to town but he did not say much about it.

About the time I was going to leave to go to my cousin's my father came into the house and told me I was not going anywhere. When I asked why he said, "If you cannot learn to listen you cannot help out at anyone else's home either." I could not understand what he was talking about so I asked him to explain and his only comment was, "You had no business going to town this morning." "Furthermore you had better plan on staying home on Sunday evening also." He sent my brother to help out at my cousin's house for the weekend.

My father was apparently very angry with me, but I had no idea why. I asked my mother for an explanation of the cruel punishment and she said, "I don't know Anna, just consider yourself lucky that your father is not as bad as his father was."

I was livid, how does this explain anything to me? Quite simply my mother blamed it all on "Dad is having a bad day and there is nothing we can do about it." I never did get an explanation from my parents. I can't say for sure if my father ever used this type of punishment on any of my other siblings, but not that I remember.

I think sometimes my father purposely let me do something he did not approve of so he could later use it to punish me, which I believe helped him get rid of his own frustrations.

Emotional abuse was very common in our family and our community. I was made to feel guilty all the time. Barely a day would go by without feeling guilty about something that I did or said. But I also truly believe that my parents disciplined my siblings and me just as they were disciplined. However, that is not an excuse to be abusive. I certainly don't use this type of discipline on my children today.

My husband and I discussed this issue shortly after we were married. We both agreed and promised each other that to never allow this kind of behavior to be a part of my family.

Human instincts tell us to play those old tapes and act upon old habits whenever something in our current life triggers old thoughts and feelings. The first step in changing those old habits is to be aware of what you are doing. And then of course taking action will certainly change old habits.

If you're angry at a loved one, hug that person. And mean it. You may not want to hug - which is all the more reason to do so. It's hard to stay angry when someone shows they love you, and that's precisely what happens when we hug each other.

~WALTER ANDERSON, THE CONFIDENCE COURSE, 1997

From The Inside Looking Out

I n my opinion the Amish are lacking education. New parents are not educated on good discipline. It seems like most of mainstream America has moved on and found better ways of disciplining the children. Although the Amish live in America, they have not adapted those new habits.

As much as they justify their actions because it was what they were taught, it still does not make it right. They are lacking love and respect for each other. Many of my cousins have left the Amish culture for the same reasons that I have. They don't feel the love and respect that they deserve.

It is so sad to say but more and more of the young are leaving the Amish culture behind to seek a happier life filled with love and respect.

Do you like how you are disciplining your children? Are your children good listeners?

I wanted my parents to listen to my side of the story. I argued because it was important to me to get my point across. So if you find yourself in an argument with your child always remember to find out the child's point of view. Sometimes you may need to take the time later to find out exactly what the argument was all about but make sure to find out.

What good comes from hitting a child and sending him/her out of sight? If only my parents would have taken the time to explain to me what and why I did wrong and needed this punishment. Talk to your children and they will thank you for the rest of your life for it.

The Secrets To Help You Thrive After Emotional Abuse

How does a person get to the point of saying, Mom, Dad I forgive you and I love you very much, after all that has happened.

First of all when I left my culture, church, and family behind I made the decision to not be a product of my upbringing. If I ever had children of my own I would learn new ways to discipline them.

The healing process started by me becoming aware of my thoughts. I stopped blaming my parents every time something went wrong. I accepted responsibility for my own actions.

I learned from my own mistakes by writing down what I did not like. It just stuck with me better and helped me to not make the same mistake twice when I wrote it down.

Also, I stopped expecting so much from other people. Within the Amish community I made my decisions based upon what I thought someone else was expecting of me and what I expected of them. Not long after I left the Amish culture I knew I had to change my thought process if I wanted my life to change.

I was willing to entertain new thinking processes. Sometimes it was as simple as finding a new way of saying something. For example, the glass is half full rather than half empty.

Don't sweat the small stuff.

Live for the moment and find something to help you enjoy each day.

CHAPTER FOUR

What Everybody Ought To Know About Name Calling

Who pays the price for demeaning comments?

A group of unmarried boys, cousins, non-cousins, and a brother (far left) at a Sunday evening gathering

Sheltered but Not Protected

Through out my years of growing up Amish I was taught it was okay to call people names. I don't think this was done intentionally but when my siblings and others in our community were allowed to call me names, I understood it was okay to do the same. Although I was crushed and felt shame, anger, unworthiness, and embarrassment every time it happened to me.

I was one of those people that tried to avoid confrontation at all costs so my come-backs were always to just laugh it off and pretend it did not bother me, and I endured the humiliation in silence. I must deserve this or God would not let it happen.

My feelings of unworthiness, anger, shame, and embarrassment were pushed as far down inside me as possible. It was the only way I knew to deal with the constant humiliation. Calling another person a nickname is a weak attempt to make one feel better while demeaning another.

Experts tell us that it takes five positive comments to correct every bad comment a child hears. Life is too short for me to receive five positive comments for every demeaning comment I received. However, these comments have taught me how to find my true feelings to overcome anything anyone wants to throw at me.

Stoney Ridge School, Hewitt MN

"The Pig"
In Grade School

My memory of the first, four years of school consists of many fun and exciting times. However there is also a very dark side that I will try to explain next.

Just a few months into my first year of school, I suddenly realized that someone at school had nicknamed me "the pig" and within a day everyone at school was using that to address me. I was devastated and cried myself to sleep that night. Now not only was my weight an issue at home; it was a huge ugly monster at school. In my eyes I was everyone's joke on a daily basis.

In first grade our school had 23 students in all which was an uneven number so when we played baseball there had to be even sides. Guess who did not get to play. Comments like, "The pig can't play, she is too fat" were daily occurrences'. I spent many recess times inside looking at and reading books or just sit outside the schoolhouse watching the rest play baseball.

I had no answers; just more questions every day. Why God why? I continued to get the same answer from my mother; the person I trusted the most. Eventually I quit asking questions. I came to the conclusion that I was born to be hated, fat, and teased no matter what. It must be my fault that all this was happening to me and not to others. I realized that food was the problem but on the other hand food was my only comfort. Literally it was the only thing I had in my life at that time that made me feel good.

Although my life seemed pretty grim at times, today I am not sorry for the experiences I given. Yes, it was not fun and especially not for a child, but it certainly has helped me to cope with challenges that I face today.

"If God brings me to it, God will help me through it." I am a much stronger person as a grown up because my childhood was not all peaches and cream.

In first, second, and third grade our reading books were all about Dick, Jane, Sally, and Spot. We learned the alphabet and then it was time to start reading. The first word I learned to read was

"Look". I remember that inner feeling of power when I was able to read. If I can read that one word, than I can read many more.

I loved every subject we studied in school. Math was a little more of a challenge, but reading, spelling, history and geography were my favorite. A couple of years I was awarded a prize at the end of the year for getting 100% in spelling. Those accomplishments helped me have a few moments to feel as if though I had the world by the tail and nothing could stop me. I will be able to do anything I want to do.

Remembering these happy moments proved to be very helpful quite a few years later in my life. This is how I survived; I hung on the good times and moved forward to my dreams.

The Truth About Teenagers – Amish or Not

I have no right, by anything I do or say, to demean a human being in his own eyes. What matters is not what I think of him; it is what he thinks of himself. To undermine a man's self-respect is a sin.

~Antoine de Saint-Exupery

When I was a teenager and my grade school nickname was no longer in existence and I was beginning to feel happier about my life in general. I was old enough to join the young folk's group.

Yes, the constant humiliation was still there but I had learned how to deal with that by creating a shell around me. This protected me from getting hurt any further and it did not matter what anyone said, I ignored it. Just when I was beginning to wonder if I had been all wrong about living in the Amish culture, I was hit with another nickname.

Barrel O' Fun was my second nickname while I grew up Amish. For a couple of weeks I was trying to figure out how those words became associated with me. Then it hit me and for days I was so sad and depressed I could hardly concentrate on anything else I was doing.

I was devastated when I realized at seventeen years old that I had not outgrown having a nickname. And most of all a demeaning nickname.

The reason this name was chosen is because when I was being teased, I would laugh and make another joke to add to the conversation; this representing "fun". My size represented "barrel". From that someone decided that since I was a bigger framed person than most of the girls that Barrel O' Fun was a perfect nickname for me.

Knowing that I had another nickname brought back many sad memories of when I was in grade school and it was not a fun time for me. I was a teenager and it should have been the best time of my life, however, again I found a coping strategy and learned how to apply it everyday.

I did not understand the why but I decided to stop asking why and search for protection instead.

The only protection I found was to build a hard shell around me which would prevent me from caring about what anyone said or did to me.

Again I say, "A fat comment or nickname is a weak attempt to make you feel better while demeaning someone else." Who pays the price for this kind of activity? Is it the person receiving the comments or the person giving the comments? In most cases both will have some kind of consequences, but in our Amish community those kinds of comments were so common that I believe only the person receiving the comments paid the price.

This experience certainly has shed some light into my life as an adult. Nicknames can be very hurtful for anyone, not just children. My children do not have nicknames, nor will I allow them to call each other nicknames, harmful or harmless.

I have greater awareness of the words I or my children use on a daily basis. I learned to have compassion for others; meet people at their own level. And do not assume anything about anyone.

How did I get past the scars that these horrible nicknames brought upon me? Like any life-changing event, it did not come easily. However, at times the only thing that mattered to me was my dreams.

I dreamt of a life free of fat comments and full of love and respect. The people in my life could call me names but they could not take away my dreams.

My first step was to truly believe that I did not deserve those nicknames. Once I got past that then I was able to focus on my faith and self respect. You will believe what you tell yourself. So tell yourself that you do not deserve this.

The next step is to find someone to talk to about how you feel. You are not designed to handle your life problems alone. If you don't have anyone in your family, find a friend or a therapist.

I found a friend to confide in; that's when the healing began. Everyone needs a friend; someone that is willing to listen even when they do not have any answers for you.

The individual woman is required... a thousand times a day to choose either to accept her appointed role and thereby rescue her good disposition out of the wreckage of her self-respect, or else follow an independent line of behavior and rescue her self-respect out of the wreckage of her good disposition.

~JEANNETTE RANKIN

Killer Secrets
To A Happy Life

In a perfect world fat comments would not exist, however we don't live in a perfect world. Everyone wants to be accepted and loved. Why was I so focused on being accepted rather than accepting myself? God has uniquely designed me so why is that not good enough?

Accepting yourself for who you are. You are a creation and gift from God not only to your parents but also to you. When I truly believed this it was the turning point for me. It is amazing what self acceptance can do.

Secondly, when I changed my belief system my thought habits changed. You only have in your life what you think about the most. If you want to change something in particular; start thinking what your life would be like when you achieve that goal. Bring that feeling of accomplishment to the core of your being. Picture you life in it for real. Life became so much easier. It took a lot less energy to have happier thoughts than to think about all the sad times.

Once I started this process I began to have some really good days. So then I wanted more and more. Eventually I forgot to go back and dwell on the sad times.

Some days were very challenging but whenever that happened I stopped my thoughts and remembered my dreams. Working through the rough days is not always easy but being patient is also a very valuable asset. Remember to have patience and be kind to yourself. This is a process so just trust that you are following it even though the future is unknown. Most of the time not knowing the future is in your best interest.

Live for the present and focus on the future.

A Day In The Life Of An Amish Girl

I n my growing up years I think our focus as a family was too much on everyone's short-comings. But I have to also remember that my parents were passing tradition on down the line. That is how they grew up so they did not know any different.

Some of those traditions are very valuable to me today. I was taught to work hard to survive. Five AM was time to get out of bed and do chores. At one point we were milking forty cows by hand, which meant I had to milk at least four or five. My siblings and I would challenge each other by timing how quickly we could fill the bucket with milk. If I milked fast enough I could build a fair amount of foam. The more foam you could get the better a milker you were.

Chore time was like a family gathering in the barn. Quite often we sang songs or we had group discussions. We would discuss the weekend happenings; who dated who or we would hear adventures my brothers sometimes had while working for non-Amish farmers.

Our routine was much the same every day. Do chores twice a day; eat three meals a day; breakfast, dinner, and supper. House chores consisted of washing dishes, sweep the floor everyday and sometimes twice a day, keep the fires going in the woodstove all day during the winter, baking and preparing meals.

At ten years old I learned how to sew. In my first sewing experience my mother let me sew a quilt together. I cut the squares from scrap materials which meant it will be multi colored. After I had sewed all the squares together my father took some pieces of wood and made a frame for me to pin it into. Then I hand-quilted it and sewed the binding around the edge. The quilt was only doll bed size but I was pretty proud of it.

I still have that quilt today. It is part of my legacy. My daughter thinks it is pretty cool to have this quilt to cover her own dolls now.

Doing dishes was one of my chores. I first started doing dishes at six years old, before I was old enough to go to school. During the years I went to school it was my job to make sure the dishes were completely done before I left for school in the morning.

After school it was my chore to wash the lunch dishes (that my mother had stacked) before supper and then again after supper.

I don't know how or why it became my duty to do dishes but it did. I am sure it did not hurt me to have that chore. I guess it taught me that sometime we all have to do things we don't like to. Doing dishes is still not one of my favorite things to do today...... go figure. That is part of the reason I have a dish washer in my kitchen today.

CHAPTER FIVE

Breakthrough Secrets *on* Facing Fear

*How would your life be today
without childhood fears?*

Anna's sister in everyday dress

Real Fears to Unreal Expectations... Can You Relate

Many moments I was scared out of my wits. Why did my parents let these things happen and continue to happen? Why did it feel like the end of the world was always in my next step? Why did my sibling get so much joy in seeing me scared to the point of crying for help?

My fears were so huge that I let them be known, which only worsened the situation. I had no defense and I didn't know how to protect myself any other way.

I was constantly being picked on, teased, and humiliated. Why God would let me be born just so bad things can happen to me and nobody cared enough to make it stop.

I was a child; I did not have enough knowledge to know that letting my fears known will only make each situation worse. Yes, kids are cruel to each other but because of my experiences in the past; today I will step in and do all I can to stop the situation when my children or other children tell me they are scared. Those fears are real and demeaning. The situation is not helpful to any child.

Are You Afraid Of the Dark

*There are very few monsters
who warrant the fear we have of them.*

~ANDRE GIDE

While I was growing up Amish I had an enormous fear of the dark. I could not stand being in darkness. One of my sibling's favorite games to play was hide-and-seek in the dark but I hated it. If I was in darkness I always felt like someone was following me and I was not going to be able to out-run my invisible stalker. My heart would beat really fast and my adrenalin would go into "fight or flight" mode. Why was my fear so huge?

Our mind works in very mysterious ways. At times it seemed like the end of my world was in my next step or just around the next corner.

Growing up Amish meant that we did not have indoor bathrooms. Utilizing the outhouse behind the house was the only option we had. I hated to go to that outhouse after dark because it always felt like someone was following me. When I looked behind me to see who was there, I could not find anyone. Quite simply my mind was telling me someone was following me when in reality there wasn't.

This experience taught me to be compassionate and understanding when others express fears to me, regardless how small the fear may be. Childhood fears are real and it is my duty as a parent to help my children understand their own fears. Talk about the fear and how you can help them overcome its power.

Are Your Fears Real or Imagined

Obstacles are like wild animals. They are cowards but they will bluff you if they can. If they see you are afraid of them... they are liable to spring upon you; but if you look them squarely in the eye, they will slink out of sight.

~ORISON SWETT MARDEN

Our school was located 1 ¼ mile from our home. Our transportation to and from school was our feet. Walking was very good for all of us, but the horrible fears of the neighbor's dogs that I experienced were not so good. A couple of homes along that road had dogs that were very bothersome for me.

Our neighbors were very nice people and I am sure they had no idea how absolutely frightened I was of their dogs. At first I was not really afraid of the dogs but then my brother had gotten bitten by one of them. After that I was absolutely petrified to walk that distance alone.

Many nights I woke up in night sweats because of nightmares about being bitten by dogs. I developed a rash on my arms and the back of my head and my hands and my feet all because my nerves were completely shot.

I guess God was watching out for me because I never did get bitten by those dogs. Every night in my prayers I thanked God for getting me through yet another day. This experience has taught me that I need to pay attention to what my children are telling me. If they have fears, I do not have the right to belittle those fears. What can I do to educate them about those fears or how can I help the situation.

I begged for my mother to understand that my fear of those dogs was very real and I wanted her to help me. I am sure my mother had no idea this experience affected me so much yet today. How could I tell her in a different way so she could understand my point of view?

As parent's, it is our job to know what is going on in our children's lives. The best way to do this is ask questions. Ask the children to tell you what they are thinking.

As I reflect back to those fear-filled days I am pretty sure I exaggerated the enormity of my fears. In other words I put a lot of energy into worrying about the dogs and trying to avoid them rather than asking for help from my siblings. But I also believed at that time; if I asked for help that meant that I was a weak person and my family did not view that as a good thing.

This is what I wished I had during my school age years. I wished I had someone to talk to about my fears, not only of those dogs but also of other normal day to day kind of things. Growing up in itself is not easy as we all know and not being able to talk to someone makes it even harder.

So my best advice would be to make sure you are a good friend to the young people. Don't judge them just listen and empathize with what they are telling you. They will thank you for years to come.

"Whatever you can do or dream you can, begin it.
Boldness has genius, power and magic in it.
Begin it now."

–GOETHE

Fear Is Normal....
How to Face It

What causes a person to fear?

My fears were real but also magnified by guilt. I was forced to feel guilty for being such a coward. How can I be so stupid to let my fear be known?

Fear is the unpleasant feeling of risk or danger either real or imagined. We fear something because we are not educated about it.

As a young child I had quite an imagination so it is possible that a certain percentage of my fears were imagined. However, the fear was very real to me.

How does a person overcome fear?

Spend your time and energy building courage to face your fears. Then you can understand the origin of the fear and how to displace it from your life. Don't try to get rid of fear or you will spend too much time and energy on the wrong thing.   Remember fear is normal and will always be a part of our lives no matter what age.

After I left the Amish culture my fears were quite different but often those same old feelings rose up. I studied my fears so much that they became fears no more.

I used to have a fear of speaking to a group or crowd of people. My desire and passion to teach the Amish culture to people overshadowed my fears of speaking. Now I still get nervous but I don't feel the fear that I used to.

Find the courage to face and understand your fears and you will go far in life.

Accept the fact that everyone has some level of fear every day and it is a normal process of life.

Gardening Is an Art

Every spring my father would use the horse drawn machinery to prepare about a half an acre for the garden. I loved to get my bare feet in the newly plowed dirt. I especially enjoyed planting the garden.

Our garden would consist of the following vegetables and fruits: green beans, peas, carrots, radishes, lettuce, onion, green and red peppers, corn, tomatoes, cabbage, kohlrabi, cucumbers, red beets, squash, pumpkin, muskmelon, watermelon, and we always had a strawberry and raspberry patch.

My mother would order her seeds in January and by March she would start a "hot bed" as we called it. A "hot bed" is a separate spot right next to the house on the south side (the warmest spot) where she started the tomato, cabbage, pepper, and kohlrabi seeds. Like a small greenhouse. This bed had an old window for a cover so the sun would help keep it warm on cool spring days. The seedlings would grow in the "hot bed" for about six weeks and then we transplanted them to the garden.

All of our spare time prior to canning time was spent keeping the garden clean of weeds. By mid July the canning season would begin and continue through September. Every year we canned at least one hundred quarts of green beans and another of corn. We always canned as many peas as our crop would give us. There never seemed to be extra peas.

My siblings and I loved to eat the peas raw. So sometimes we ate just as many raw as we canned. Mom would literally have to chase us out of the garden.

Rhubarb was another fruit we enjoyed. My mother had a rhubarb juice recipe that I really enjoyed. We canned the juice and then enjoyed it during the winter.

Gardening is very rewarding and I enjoy it but don't do much currently due to time constraints. I hope to find the time to enjoy this hobby again someday.

CHAPTER SIX

May I Have Your Opinion

What would be your decision?

Anna's sisters on each side and their friend in the middle

Mastering the Art Of Opinions & Decisions

While I was growing up I was taught to be seen and not heard. My opinion did not matter. My job was to do as I was told and without argument. My questions were answered with, "It is not right to ask why, you just need to do as we tell you and everything will work out okay."

Severely confused would be one way to explain my reaction. I learned to feel guilt, anger, frustration, humiliation, and etc. Love, caring, empathy, and support were not part of my vocabulary.

Not being allowed to have an opinion taught me to hate myself so much that I wanted to die from emotional pain. Who was I and why was I in this world?

For many years it was my mission to find the true me. I wanted to feel good about my decisions and be allowed to voice my opinion without being judged.......or at least not always.

However, life is hard and words can go through a person like a sharp knife, which is not a reason to want to die. Nobody promised me that life will be easy. You can have a better outlook on life just by practicing better thinking habits and taking action.

Amazing Life Changes Just By Listening

*The inability to make a decision
has often been passed off as patience.*

~AUTHOR UNKNOWN

Within the Amish culture all major decisions were made for me and any small decisions I made were based on what someone else wanted me to do. My parents never asked me for my opinion. I was taught to do as I was told without any questions or objections. My interactions with my parents and siblings were such that they did not allow me to have an opinion.

I was a very normal child, and I did voice my opinion just like any child would. The only difference is I was very quickly told that I did not have the right to have an opinion because it was not a choice. The harsh discipline from my father taught me to keep my frustrations to myself.

The Amish culture is a very male dominated culture. Yes my mother had her say in major decisions but ultimately all decisions were made by my father. My mother taught me it was okay for her to disagree with a decision my father made but it is wrong to show that disagreement in public or in front of the children. Therefore, I did not get the chance to learn how to deal with disagreements.

On the other hand I think today too many parents fight out their arguments in front of their children and that is not good. Parents need to find a middle ground for working out disagreements. My children don't need to know when I have a disagreement with my husband. We make every effort to keep our disagreements between us and only us.

But you still need to find a way to teach your children that it is okay to disagree. Teach them the technique to "Agree to disagree" and how to come to a compromise that fits for everyone. This is what I was missing in my growing up Amish.

The difference between my way of thinking and my mother's is that she sometimes did not stand up for what she thought was right; (since she was the female of the house she did not have that right) even when she totally disagreed with my father. My values and beliefs are very important to me and my husband feels the same so when we do disagree we take the time to discuss both sides and come to a compromise.

Do you have any idea what it's like to disagree in silence? I learned that technique very quickly. It was easier to know in my heart that I had a different opinion than to have another disagreement with my parents. My family could keep me from voicing my opinion, but they could not prevent me from having an opinion.

When I left the Amish culture I had to learn how to voice my opinions. So the first thing I learned was to make my own decisions. That was very hard to learn. My friend asked me, "Should we have hamburgers or hotdogs for dinner this evening?" and I always responded with "Whatever you all want, it does not matter to me."

My friend did not give up that easily. She refused to decide for me but asked that I make a decision and she would be happy with whatever I decide. Wow, at first I was very uncomfortable being forced to make a decision, but after a while it felt wonderful to know someone care about my opinion.

Who are we doing justice when we don't teach our children to make any decisions in life as they grow up? Is it stealing?

This experience has taught me that it is my duty as a parent to teach my children how to make decisions on their own. I know it would have been much easier for me to make good decisions had I gotten a chance to exercise the decision making process.

When I decided to leave that culture I thought I knew how to make good decisions, but life in a non-sheltered environment was a completely new animal. All of a sudden the consequences of my decisions were so much more prominent to me.

Very quickly I learned to remember the mistakes of prior decisions and to not make them again. Sometimes when I asked my friends for advice I did not like the answers they gave me. Then I had to decide to either follow what they told me or choose my own path.

However, I felt it was in my best interest to follow the advice of someone who had lived the unsheltered life a lot longer than I had. So when I asked for recommendations from a friend, I applied extra effort to follow them. After all, my passion was to learn how to live comfortably in this unsheltered life. With pride I can say I am very happy and content with my life today.

Now, I am no different than anyone else. I still make mistakes and I don't expect to be perfect. The only requirement is to keep trying and never give up. Life can be better if we make up our minds to make it better. A little bit of effort can go a long way if we want it.

*Courage doesn't always roar. Sometimes courage is
the little voice at the end of the day that says
I'll try again tomorrow.*

~MARY ANNE RADMACHER

CHAPTER SEVEN

20 Out *of* Every 100 Are Facing This..... Did You

The numbers are astronomical, but why?

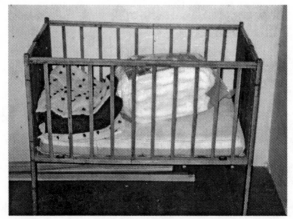

*The crib Anna's mother used for all 10 babies
and now for her grandchildren*

Religious Or Not The Numbers Are The Same

Why would God let this happen to me? What on earth did I do to deserve this? I felt angry, ashamed, dirty, and humiliation during this horrible event in my life.

It must be my fault because my parents blamed me for every incident. How could I stop this horrible abuse when I did not have the right to object?

My way of coping was to shut down and quit trying to figure out why bad things happened to me. I pushed all the pain as far down inside me as possible. I built a hard shell around me to protect the little dignity I still had.

Nobody is deserving of this abuse. It was the worst thing that ever happened to me. Years after this horrible experience I realized that I had an enormous amount of faith all throughout. Otherwise I would not be here today. When others in our community found out what was happening, I then had to deal with more humiliation.

I will never again give another person that kind of control over me. But remember I was only eight years old at the time.

It took me years to realize that life is too short to dwell on what could have been. I needed to stop beating myself up for what I did not know back then. I came to the conclusion that I did the best I knew how and God would not ask any more of me ever.

It's Not Your Fault
You Know

*The moment a man claims a right to control
the will of a fellow being by physical force,
he is at heart a slaveholder.*

~Henry C. Wright, The Liberator, 7 April 1837

This chapter of my life is written with a heavy heart. I want my readers to understand that there were many happy times in our family, but there were also many sad and hurtful times. It is amazing how the sad and hurtful times are still so vivid in my mind. I came to the conclusion a long time ago that the sad and hurtful situations were life changing for me and that is why it is still so vivid in my memory.

When I was eight years old I was sexually molested. I was told that this was our secret and if I told anyone it would just happen again and again. I had no idea what it all meant but I did know it did not make me feel good. I also was pretty sure if I told anyone I would be blamed for it as being my fault that it happened.

The abuse went on for quite some time before I realized it was happening to one of my other siblings also. We never talked to each other about it. We just pretended it was not happening to either of us. Today I wonder why we chose not to say something to someone, but I think that was our way of dealing with this horrible situation.

Months after the abuse had begun I realized that my mom knew what was happening. Right after an incident she confronted me, wanting to know where I had been. When I told her she scolded me for going there and if I had not gone there it would not have happened. I told her I had not chosen to go but was pushed to go. I was completely devastated when she did not believe me. I could not believe I was being blamed for this and the abuser was pretty much off the hook.

My dad was not at home most every day but my mom usually was. I decided that I needed to stay close to mom so I could get by a day and not have any abuse happen, but that did not always work.

One day my mother and two older sisters had gone to another Amish family's home for the day. They did not make sure they were home by the time we got home from school. I was so mad that they had left me and my little sister at home alone. I took my little sister and went to the neighbor's cornfield and hid until I knew my mom was home.

I tried everything I knew to discourage the abuse but I was not even a teenager yet. There was not much I could do. You need to remember that the Amish culture is very male dominated and what the males want they get. I believe the person that abused me was mentally ill but nobody wanted to believe it. I tried so hard to explain that I was forced but somehow it was always my fault.

I am not sure if my parents truly believed that the sexual abuse was my fault or not but they always made me feel like I was at fault. Again I came to the conclusion that if I was not so overweight my parents would like me more and protect me from all the horrible abuse.

If only I could be the perfect person so I could be liked. God must be punishing me for not being able to control my eating habits and not doing exactly what I was supposed to. I just could not come up with any other explanation. I must be deserving of such horrible abuse.

To make matters worse one of my older siblings spread the word to other Amish families in the community about the abuse and now more people looked at me as the dirtiest, ugliest, most disgusting person on this earth.

I know some of my other siblings also endured abuse and I felt absolutely horrible for them. I don't know how but somehow they were able to silently work through the hurt and anger caused by the abuse; unlike me. I just pushed it all into the back of my mind so far so that I did not have to think about it anymore.

The abuse continued for about four years and then I decided I had had enough and was not going to put up with it anymore. I just refused to do what the abuser wanted me to do. I ran and hid; I pushed, kicked, and screamed if I needed to, to get away. Finally I was not being bothered anymore, but the scar that this horrible thing left behind took me years to heal.

There were two issues for me to come to terms with. First, I had to deal with all the hurt and anger from the abuse and I also had to deal with the anger towards my parents for letting the abuse happen. Certainly my parents must hate me a lot if they let this happen to me; but why? I could not understand why God would want me to be born, only to be hated and abused.

When bad things happened to me and I asked my mother why; she said, "Well Anna, maybe if you had only done what you were supposed to do, God would not let bad things happen to you." Therefore, I came to the conclusion that every bad thing that had ever happed to me was because I was not good enough and needed to be punished by God for it.

As sure as the sun came up every morning; I was certain that God would someday strike me dead for my evil deeds. I finally came to the point where I truly believed that if I didn't do exactly as everyone around me wanted me to; God would make something bad happen to me again.

From this experience I learned to seek for guidance from God. I didn't want this to be a part of mine or my family's life ever. Today I know that God is a loving and forgiving God and is not at all what I had in my mind during my growing up years. I am also certain that my parents did not intend to teach me that God was bad, however that is what I got from it.

For the most part I truly believe that my parents did the best they could with the knowledge they had. We must remember they did not have the option to turn the abuser in to the authorities. The Amish do not believe in getting law enforcement involved if it can absolutely be avoided.

Now that I am a parent and because of this experience, I am so much more aware of what I need to know about my children's daily lives. I need to ask and know what is going on; the good and the bad. I want my children to know that they can tell me anything and I will not throw blame and guilt at them. All the things I wanted my parents to do for me is foremost in my thoughts as I parent my children.

There is always something good that you can take from bad experience. I didn't used to believe that but I decided I will not be a product of my upbringing (by that I mean I will live by different values than I was taught). I will be a product of my own decisions. Life is great and I feel very content and happy.

> *We must remain as close to the flowers, the grass, and the butterflies as the child is who is not yet so much taller than they are. We adults, on the other hand, have outgrown them and have to lower ourselves to stoop down to them. It seems to me that the grass hates us when we confess our love for it. Whoever would partake of all good things must understand how to be small at times.*
>
> ~FRIEDRICH NIETZSCHE

Secrets to Thrive After the Ultimate Pain

F orgiveness is very powerful.

Now some may wonder how I can forgive something as painful as this.

For many years I blamed the abuser and my parents for what happened and I carried that anger with me. Only the people that this has happened to truly have any idea what a heavy load that is.

A couple of years after I left the Amish culture I decided I was no longer going to give the abuser and my parents that power over me. When you carry the guilt, anger, and frustration with you; it is not only a heavy load, but you are also giving that person the power.

Letting go of the guilt and anger was not easy but it was the best thing I could do. I am telling you I felt like a cat let out of a plastic bag.

Now I could move forward and those old tapes would stop playing over and over in my mind. I wanted to get rid of that and struggled to find out how; but it was quite simple.

After that, anytime my thoughts went back to the fear of forgiveness I forced my brain to stop thinking that way and remembered how wonderful it felt to be free.

Forgive and you will be free!

CHAPTER EIGHT

Intimacy *and* Amish Culture…..Do They Mix

Do you live your dream or someone else's?

Anna's sister and former boyfriend

A Startling Realization.... A Miracle To Recognize It

Time passed by very slowly and I could not wait to be old enough to have my own home, family, and life. It is every Amish girl's dream to get married and have a family.

I was very enthusiastic, energetic and felt like I had the world by the tail. As the years went by my dreams were crushed. Demeaning remarks, low self esteem, and a weekly reminder of how incompetent I was, is enough to crush anyone's dreams.

The tiny bit of self confidence that I had I lost very quickly. I became very depressed, and again I just wanted to die. It is not surprising that I did not find true love. How can someone else love me if I don't love me?

This is a very important tip so pay attention. If you don't show love for your children they may not learn how to love themselves.

That is what I was missing. I did not know how to love myself. I was very abusive to my body and mind and I truly believed that was the only way to deal with the emotional pain I was experiencing.

How could I let another person have that kind of control over me? Now I can teach my children to never let others take control of their lives. I know my children will not have to overcome as many huge obstacles as I did. That is very exciting for me. Life is good if we decide to make it that way.

How To Achieve
A Sense of Belonging

I walk these halls every day
In the flow of acquaintances and friends,
In this place of hundreds I try to make my way
Yet I feel so lost and out of place. Smiles greet me in
faces I know
And I can't help but smile back,
But even so my real feelings I cannot show
For the feelings of connecting escapes me.

I find myself at odds with my peers
Unable to blend in with my surroundings,
I cannot seem to quench these fears
Of not fitting in or belonging.

~Author Unknown

In my Amish community the rule was that when a person
turned sixteen and one-half years old they were allowed to join
the young folk's group.

Finally I was old enough to belong to this group. I was very excited. It was fun to get out of the house on Sunday and mingle with other young people of our community.

My greatest fear that first Sunday evening in late August was that I would never feel like I belong anywhere. Up until then this is what my life had been about. Where do I fit in and why was I here on earth?

Yep, you guessed it. My fears did come true. I never really did fit in. Years later I learned that for every thought I act upon I get a result. The metaphor certainly applied in this event in my life.

First of all, my self respect was non-existent and I certainly did not receive any respect from others in this group. Because I was now old enough, I was expected to show up wherever the young folk's group was invited to, only to be humiliated once again.

Some of the boys made fun of me the minute they realized I had joined the group. They did not know me and they had no intention of getting to know me. I believe their mentality was, "Hey now we have a new girl we can use and make fun of." It certainly confirmed my level of self respect and self worth.

Why was I put into this world for people to hate and make fun of?

In this Amish community that we lived in, I would describe life as an Amish teenager "pure hell". Constantly someone would pretend to be my friend and ask me questions and then turn around and stab me in the back with the information I provided. It didn't matter what I did or said; I was always picked on. Shortly after I had joined the group I was labeled with a nickname.

If I was being teased and picked on in front of the whole group, I would always just laugh it off (even though it was killing me inside) and make it look like it did not bother me. I certainly did not want to inconvenience anyone else. The pain would have been much less had someone just taken a knife and put it through my heart. It was the most horrible public humiliation I ever experienced.

Not having anyone to talk to, someone who would understand my feelings and thoughts was harder than you can imagine. Nobody cared enough to hear what I had to say. I was too embarrassed to share my feelings with my parents and I truly did not think it would change anything even if I had told them. My parent's answer to every question was, "If you would just do as you are supposed to, these kind of comments would not bother you any." To me that made it my fault once again.

The first four years after joining the young folk group were the worst time of my life. I was publicly embarrassed on a weekly basis and then told to quit complaining about other people and not let it bother me. I did not know how to make it stop so I continued to accept total responsibility by saying to myself, "if only I was not so fat and ugly this would not be happening to me."

Today I know God was watching over me. God did not want me to die, although I wanted to so many times. Serious thoughts to hurt or kill myself were very vivid and real in my mind, but God did not give me the courage to act upon those thoughts. That is the only reason I am still alive today.

Wouldn't It Be Nice To Know What Is Expected Of You

Being a part of the young folks group meant that I was old enough to start dating guys if I chose to do so. The young folks got together every Sunday evening. The gatherings were usually at the home of where church was held that day.

In the summer time we played volley ball and then we sang for an hour or so. After that it was a time for the guys to ask a girl for a date. Taking a girl on a date meant that the guy would give her a ride home and was allowed to spend a greater part of the night visiting with her. This activity was to take place in the living room of the girl's home. If you already had a steady girlfriend, then again this was time to take her home and spend time getting to know her better.

In our community there was an activity called "cutting up". This meant that pretty much anyone that was not going on a date would go to the homes where they knew a couple was and harass them for a while. My brothers loved this, which meant I had to come along. I always felt sorry for the couple and often wished our community would not allow others to bother them.

First of all, they had so little time to really get to know each other, and secondly, to be bothered by all who did not get a date that evening was just plain cruel or so I thought. The couple of times I had a date I was also victimized. Some of the pranks that occurred; I would call vandalism.

For example, smearing stove pipe soot all over the couples face. It got on their clothes, which is very hard to remove. Or taking the wheels off the guy's buggy and hiding them. And some used spray paint to write profanity on the barn walls.

Our community had a rule that the boys were to leave the girl's homes by 2:00 AM. Anyone who was not going on a date had to be home by 12:00 AM. Quite often these rules were not followed. Many times it was 3 or 4 AM before I and my sibling got home.

My parents usually did not hear us come home and they also did not ask us the next day what time we got home. They only asked when they were suspicious of something. Like rumors of a drinking party or someone getting caught with a radio.

Intimacy…How To Make Love Work

What is this feeling I have?
I seem to love you
But other times I seem to loathe you

I can't be without you
Or maybe just without anyone
I think about you all the time
But why do I have this feeling?

I long for your voice
And I would die to hear your laugh
But is this love
Or merely lust?

BY GARY R. HESS

Just after I turned seventeen years old, one day I received a letter in the mail from a guy from another community about 100 miles to the north. He wanted to know if I would be interested in a long distance relationship. This pretty much meant we got to know each other through writing letters.

I was in complete shock. How is it possible that another human being could actually think of me as someone he would like to get to know and could possibly fall in love with? I took a couple of days to think about it and read the letter over and over.

I had met this guy at my sisters wedding a couple of months prior but I didn't know anything about him. I was very hesitant and scared but decided to take a leap of faith and get to know this person more. We began exchanging letters on a weekly basis. Finally I had an interest outside of our community; something I could focus on, and it felt really good to know that someone in this world was interested in me and how I felt.

He came to visit a couple of months after our first contact. He was really nice and I enjoyed his company. The minute my cousins saw him they were making fun of his appearance. He was very normal to me but he did have reddish hair. I did not have enough self esteem not to care what they thought. It really bothered me how self centered and narrow minded some of my cousins were.

We continued to exchange letters and visited when ever we could. When we visited each other's homes we had more time to get to know each other. Sometimes we would visit all night because that was when we had privacy. After dating for two years I started to feel that maybe this was not the man for me. I could not really come up with a reason why I felt that way, but it just did not feel right anymore. I prayed to God to show me what to do, and eventually I decided to break up with him and follow whatever God wanted me to do; I did not have any idea what that was.

A couple of weeks went by and I decided that I missed him too much. I sent him a letter asking for a second chance and he was willing to give me that. By now I was almost nineteen and I went to visit him for the Christmas holiday. He proposed to me during my visit and I accepted.

When I came home I asked my parents if we could get married in the spring. I was told no, spring was too soon and if we still wanted to get married we could do so in the fall. This upset me very much. Their reason for saying no was they could not afford the cost in the spring but would try to by fall. Pretty much the same answer I always got when I asked for anything. Again they had found a way to say no when I wanted something.

I told my boyfriend and he understood why I was upset but he was okay with the idea that we would get married in September. Our wedding plans were well underway. My mother in law to-be had found some dark blue fabric which she gave to me for my wedding dress. I accepted the fabric but also realized that she had purchased that fabric for me so she had control of what I would be wearing for my wedding.

I prayed to God to help me feel loved and show me how to love this person but it just did not happen. Why was it so easy for my sisters and other girls in the community to seem happy? Why was I getting unhappier as each day passed and more wedding plans were made? I thought I was so in love with this guy and I truly wanted to marry him. It took me years to realize that God was watching me and had my best interest in mind when he did not answer my prayers. Obviously I was not following God's plan for me.

I spent many hours thinking about our wedding day; how beautiful it could be and how happy I will make this guy I thought I loved. My greatest fear was that our wedding day would be a disaster if others from my community were allowed to tease and humiliate me as they did on any other day. My mind was filled with thoughts of worse case possible. How am I going to get through this day with any dignity left?

Eventually I was looking for ways to have our wedding in his community. I asked my boyfriend if we could have the wedding at his parent's house. Of course he was very accepting of that and so were his parents. However, my parents simply said no. "If you can't get married here, there will not be a wedding." I was not surprised by their answer, because again the answer was no when I wanted something.

Because of my dysfunctional relationship with my parents, I was not able to clearly explain why I wanted our wedding moved to another community. I did not get a chance to explain my true feelings. Eventually I could not find a way around my huge mound of fears so I decided to break up with my boyfriend to avoid having to get married in our community.

Today I believe God was watching over me and getting married to an Amish guy was not part of the plan. I felt so relieved when I had broken up with my boyfriend and I could stop the wedding plans. On one hand I was finally free of something I did not want to do, but on the other hand now I did not have an outside interest to focus on and I could not see a way to get away from this community.

I talked to my mom about all the things I did not like that were happening in our community and she said, "Maybe if you followed the rules better good things would come to you." I did not argue with her nor did I believe her. She had told me that for many years now and nothing had changed. I did not know if I would ever figure out who I was and if there was any place here on earth that I would fit in.

It is every Amish girl's dream to find a partner you can fall in love with and then be the best wife and mother you can be. When

I turned 20 years old I was told by my disrespectful cousins that I was the "old maid" of the community and I would never find anyone that could like me or for sure never live with me. Hearing someone actually say those horrible things to me was hard enough, but I heard disrespectful comments often enough that I believed every word I heard.

I spent many hours taking inventory of all the demeaning and horrible things that either happened to me or were said to me. I came to the conclusion that they were all true. I was worthless, unlovable, unlikable, fat and the ugliest person in the whole world. I hated me just as much as others told me they hated me.

I had built a hard shell around me to protect me from getting hurt anymore. This was the only way for me to have any control of my feelings.

So how do you make love work?

The only way to make love work is first and foremost be true to yourself. Don't live by what you hear others say and certainly don't put your energy into living someone else's dream for you.

What is your dream? My dream was to live a life of feeling content with myself and a sense of belonging. Having a boyfriend and going through all the motions of a wedding would not have brought that to me.

I thank God for showing me that prior to marrying this person I did not truly love. My inner spirit was in control and I just needed to listen to it.

> *In everyone's life, at some time, our inner fire goes out.*
> *It is then burst into flame by an encounter with another*
> *human being. We should all be thankful for those people*
> *who rekindle the inner spirit.*
>
> ~Albert Schweitzer

Insider Secrets You Won't Want To Miss

A very common question I receive from my audiences is: Are the marriages' arranged by your parents? There are some cultures where all marriages are arranged but Amish are not one of them. As far as I know arranged marriages has never been a tradition in the Amish culture. However, there are rigorous rules that do apply during your search for a life partner.

* Dating was not allowed until you are at least sixteen years old. In some communities dating was not allowed until seventeen years of age. In my community the rule was sixteen and one half years old. Dating does not start in grade school. Dating someone from outside the Old Order Amish churches was also not allowed.

* First dates are done with as much secrecy as possible. The guy will send a close friend to ask the girl he wants to take on a date that evening. This is all done after a Sunday evening gathering

in the privacy of darkness. The guy then gives the girl a ride home to spend a couple of hours getting to know her. If he likes her he may ask her for a second date the next weekend. Girls do not ask guys for dates.

Since I dated someone from another community our first date in person was a little different, but the same rules applied. We had exchanged letters via mail weekly for almost two months when he came to visit for the day. When dusk arrived that evening, we escaped the front yard by going for a walk just so we could have some privacy. Public affection was not practiced. In fact if a couple did show some public affection it would become the news of the week.

My boy friend's home was one hundred miles from our home, so when he visited he would usually stay for a couple of days. Sometimes we would visit and get to know each other most of the night. Living in a household of ten people proved to be a challenge to find privacy for any length of time.

* A couple cannot get married until they become members of the church. To become a member you need to attend classes and be baptized. After you are a member; when you get married is pretty much up to you, your partner, and the parents involved. Some of the girls get married as young as seventeen years old.

* The Amish do not baptize babies. They believe in adult baptism. I was baptized when I was eighteen years old. A person cannot become a member of the Amish church until you have attended a series of classes where they teach you the rules and beliefs of the church.

After completing the classes, I prepared for my baptismal day. I wore all new clothes, which was the extent of any celebration that occurred. Baptism takes place during church services. The Bishop asked me to kneel on the floor and respond to each question with "I do". When that was complete the bishop's wife came and took my cap off my head. Next the bishop poured small amounts of water on my head while saying, "I baptize you in the name of the Father, Son, and Holy Ghost." Next my cap was placed back on my head and the bishop's wife took my hand and I got back up on my feet and we sealed it with a kiss.

* The decision to get married is solely on the couple itself. Sometimes the parents will have some rules for their children to follow, but the parents want to see their children grow up and get married within the Amish church. Once a couple decides to get married, all communication about the wedding between the two families is done through the couple. The wedding is usually at the bride's home.

* A honeymoon is not part of a newly married Amish couple's celebrations. When my oldest sister was married, her and her new husband helped clear out the tables, sort and return dishes to the rightful owners, and move furniture back into our home the next couple of days. Before they were married one week, we had packed up all their belongings and they moved to the home where they planned to live and real married life began.

* Birth control is not practiced within the Amish churches. Women will have as many children as they can prior to menopause. There aren't any rules as to how many children you can have. The only rule that does exist is that it is sinful to practice birth control.

Anna with a cigarette and a wine cooler,
and a younger sister

Do You Have God on One Shoulder and the Devil on the Other

This chapter is about some of the fun things I was involved in while growing up Amish.

A year or two after I joined the young folks group at sixteen and one half years old I felt quite a lot of peer pressure to get into activities that I knew would not make my parents happy. The young folks group met every Sunday evening and usually by ten pm it should have been time to go home. However, a select group of teenagers felt it was party time instead.

While speaking to audiences I get asked, "Is it true that when the boys and girls turn 16, they go on all-night parties and drink, dance, smoke and have sex? Then they can decide if they want to stay out of the culture or go back?"

Believe it or not.....this has been told as a true fact within the Amish culture. It really amazes me what is written as Amish tradition. I grew up in this lifestyle and have never known this to be true, at least not in the community I lived in. Yes we had drinking parties, smoked cigarettes, and enjoyed country music; however, I did not have my parents' permission to attend these parties.

Amish teenagers are no different than teenagers in any other culture. We wanted to experience some of those unwanted behaviors but dancing and staying out all night were not an option. Sometimes it was pretty late when we got home, but that simply meant we got less sleep that night. We still had to get up at 5:30 am to do chores and continue the Monday work just like any other day.

In the community that I grew up these parties were always done in a very secretive fashion. We paid much attention to who was in attendance because some of the kids were well known to attend parties and then talk about it all week to anyone they came in contact with. This meant everyone at the party was going to get in trouble (be shunned and have to ask for forgiveness in front of the whole church).

Someone from our party group had a boom box so we could enjoy music and everyone brought their own drinks. Mostly these parties would take place outside after dark in some field or wooded area where we would not be seen from the roadway. Winter time made it difficult to have parties outdoor's, so we enjoyed the summertime when it was warm out.

It seemed like someone was always getting caught with having liquor, a radio, or a camera. All of these were not allowed according to the rules of the church. If you were a member (already baptized) or not a member (not baptized yet).

We were teenagers and going on these parties was our way of acting out. We did not have our parents' consent and it meant trouble and humiliation of the whole church knowing what you did if you got caught. I did get caught one time but I also did not hesitate to lie about many of my actions when I was questioned about it.

As the years went by, I began to realize how hypocritical I had become. With my Amish clothes and lifestyle I was professing to be a Christian, but my actions were not Christian at all. I realized that I needed to find a way to better myself; Amish or not Amish. The more I questioned the church rules and wanted to know why on specific issues, the more I realized that living Amish was no longer going to be for me.

How had my life become so two sided. I felt I had God one shoulder and the Devil on the other. The Devil was telling me to keep doing what I was doing and God was telling me that I knew better and huge changes needed to occur to stop all the lying and deceitful actions. I felt like I was between a rock and a cement wall.

If I left the Amish culture I was going to disappoint many people and most of all my parents. If I stayed I was so scared that my depression would take over, I would not stop abusing my own body and in the process I would end up killing myself to stop the pain I was feeling.

Obviously God was in control during all this time. Many times I just wanted to die to stop the emotional pain that I was experiencing but I never had the courage to fiscally hurt my body. Then I was introduced to my friends Penny and Jon who were there to help me leave the Amish culture and find a better way of life.

These experiences were just another stepping stone in the plan God had for me. My next book will be about my transition years and how I worked my way through to this side.

CHAPTER NINE

Fact You Should Know About Major Losses

Do you blame yourself when you experience a loss?

Where Anna lived the last 8 years of Amish life

How To Deal With....
A Home Lost By Fire

I was certain that God was punishing my family for my actions. I was the cause for this horrible fire. Also my mother said, "If we didn't have things in our home that were just for show and pride, God would not let a fire destroy our home."

I felt so guilty for having unnecessary, materialistic items in my bedroom that would cause God to let this happen to us. Like a large mirror; 16x20 in size with some small pattern on it; our dishes were arranged nicely on the dresser and shelf; and we had blue curtains on the windows.

I reflected back to what I had done and how I could change things. I also wondered why it was my fault once again. God must really hate me if he destroyed our home to get my attention.

Yes, events happen for a reason but sometimes it is nobody's fault. Why does it always have to be someone's fault? Because this happened to me, I was able to find the true love of God, that he really does care, and God is not this monster I used to think he was.

Did You Know....
When One Door Closes
Another Opens

To bring up a child in the way he should go, travel that way yourself once in a while.

~JOSH BILLINGS

I n April of 1984 on a Saturday afternoon our house caught on fire. That day we had a strong wind from the east and the fire started on the west end of the house roof. Our house was old and had wooden shingles on the roof.

My little sisters were outside playing in the yard when they saw the roof was on fire. They ran to the house to tell my mom and older sisters. One of my older sisters immediately ran to the neighbors to call the fire department. My dad had gone to town to get some groceries when he saw the fire trucks leave town; not realizing the fire trucks were coming to our house. Someone in town heard where the fire trucks were going and told my dad he had better go home, which he did.

The cause of the fire was determined to be from our wood stove in the living room. Since it was fairly warm outside that day my mother did not have much fire going in the stove. Apparently the east wind was strong enough to create a back suction up through the chimney; sucking live coals from the stove and they fell on the roof which had wooden shingles.

The fire department did get to the fire in time to save some of our belongings that were in the living room. However, the fire destroyed most everything that was upstairs; everything in mine and my sisters' room was either burned completely or melted to a pile beyond recognition. The boys' closet was still intact but their clothes were partially melted and smelled of smoke so much that we could not salvage any. There was very little damage in the master bedroom on the main floor and most everything in the kitchen only had water damage.

I was helping out at a cousin's house that week, so I didn't know about the fire and that all my personal belongings were gone until the next day about noon. I was absolutely devastated; I cried for hours. When I walked into the burned house to check it out I was absolutely overwhelmed with grief, extreme sadness, anger, frustration, and relief that nobody had gotten hurt and we were all safe. I felt so lost; where would we go from here without a home big enough to live in. Thank goodness our farm had a second small house.

On Sunday evening after I saw the devastation of the fire, I was asked to go back to my cousin's house to help out that next week. I didn't want to go but mom said yes, which gave me no choice but to go. At home on Monday morning they prepared the small house for my family to live in until we could rebuild.

This little house was too small to provide sleeping space for everyone, so my parents and three younger sisters slept in the small house.

My brothers slept in the front porch of the big house (the porch had only a little water damage) which had a door to the outside, and my two older sisters and I slept in the master bedroom of the big house. That bedroom had a door to the outside also so none of us had to go through the burned structure to get to our sleeping quarters. That is how we lived for the rest of that summer.

Since we did not have fire insurance through an Insurance company, we relied on the other church districts to help pay for rebuilding costs. If I remember correctly there were 6 other districts that helped.

A few members (usually male) that are not personally connected to the loss or illness are asked to determine what the cost is and then let each district know how much they are expected to pay. Then someone from each district will give each family a slip of paper telling them how much they owe and where to send the money.

Within a month, clean up and rebuilding began. Throughout the month of June we had building crews to feed almost on a daily basis. Sometimes some of the women came from the community to help cook for the men at work. Otherwise that is what my sisters and I got done each day; spend all morning cooking a big meal and then clean up in the afternoon and prepare more food for the next day.

Some of the structure of the house was salvageable. The upstairs was completely torn off and rebuilt. This gave us the ability to expand the upstairs. Before the fire, we had three bedrooms upstairs and now there would be five. On the main floor most of the outside walls and windows were reused; the old siding was torn off and the inside was gutted and redone. During a previous remodeling job a lot of paneling was used which was now torn out and we put up sheetrock.

We worked hard all summer and by mid October we moved into our newly built home. There was still quite a bit of finishing work to be done inside, but winter was coming so we moved in and did the finishing work later. I was very excited to have more bedrooms upstairs

I was taught when bad things happen to me it was because I was not following the rules of our home or the church and God was punishing me for my bad actions.

Can you even imagine the level of guilt now that our home was gone? How could I change my thoughts so that God would not have to punish us anymore?

Certainly I was the cause for this horrible fire. Also my mother said, "If we didn't have things in our home that were just for show and pride, God would not let a fire destroy our home."

Loosing our home was hard, but it also taught me that when one door closes another one will open. I just needed to have faith and be thankful that everyone was okay. Materialistic things are just that and should not be the basis of our being. We don't always have total control of what happens.

We don't always know when or how the other door will open, but for me I just needed to be patient. Many doors opened for me in the years to come.

I also learned that God was not punishing me. However, I began to realize how important life is and how quickly it can change. I needed to live every day as if it is my last day here on earth.

*"Love like you will never get hurt
and dance like nobody is watching"*

-AUTHOR UNKNOWN

Do You Carry Guilt......Why

How does a person overcome the huge amount of guilt that we tend to carry on our shoulders every day?

Within the Amish community I was taught that every accident or mishap that occurred was for a reason. So quite frankly there were no accidents or mishaps. Right?

The people in my community found a reason for everything. For example: a young man had left our community and one morning while driving to work he fell asleep at the wheel, missed a curve and was killed in a rollover car accident.

There were many comments and reasons throughout the community why this person was killed. It was the talk of the town for awhile.

Many used it as an example: saying to their young, "Now you can see what can happen when you leave. God must have been punishing him for leaving." Others voiced their opinion saying, "God must be punishing his parents for not teaching him better ways."

There had to be a reason for everything. That is what I experienced at home too. When my oldest brother left the Amish my mother blamed herself. God was punishing her for her wrong doings.

It took me quite some time to realize that I am not to blame for every accident or mishap that occurs in my life.

Again I practiced being aware of my thoughts. Accepting what has happened and moving forward is the key to getting beyond all the guilt. Don't live in fear of what might happen in the future.

Learn from your past. Live for the present.

Each day find something nice and beautiful in your life. You may be surprised how much you can find if you look. I know I certainly was able to find lots to be thankful for when I really looked. And everyday I could find more and more. Life is good if we want it that way.

CHAPTER TEN

Where Did Anna Go Next

*Life is a journey so come along as I
share the best of both worlds.*

Anna dressed for church

CONCLUSION

*"Children are likely to live up
to what you believe of them."*

~LADY BIRD JOHNSON

I HOPE YOU HAVE ENJOYED reading about my journey as I grew up Amish as much as I did writing it.

My dream is to be an inspiration to others as you learn what my life was like Growing up Amish. I had to overcome some obstacles and that was not easy. At times I felt that life would never get any better and I was doomed to hell for my actions. But somehow I was always able to know that quitting was not an option and I needed to continue my struggles for a better way of life. I truly believe God's Angels were walking with me in guidance.

Many days I wished I had the courage to disappear into the woods somewhere and never be seen again. That was how low my life was at times. But I could not find the courage so it is quite clear to me that God was watching.

I would guess my journey is not so different than many of my readers. If there is something in your life that you don't like, apply a little of your energy every day to change it. That is what it took for me to change my life. At times it did not seem like my efforts were fruitful, but over time I began to see good changes.

All the events I talk about in this book happened before I was seventeen years old. The next book; COMING SOON; I share the mindset I had to have for me to get to the point of leaving the Amish culture. How that affected me, how I felt about it at the time, and how it has changed my life forever.

I look forward to sharing more of my journey in my next book "The Five Steps of Leaving".

Do you belong to a group who would like to hear my story or want to ask me questions? Please don't hesitate to contact me. I will come and talk to your group and at these speaking engagements I always leave time to interact with my audience. You get to ask me any question you like. I love sharing what I experienced and talking to people.

Contact me at www.GrowingUpAmish.com/public.htm for a customized program just for your group and special pricing.

For more of my journey make sure to visit.

www.GrowingUpAmish.com

Anna's sister dressed for church

By now you may be wondering what happened to Anna, how did she survive the transition from Amish to the unsheltered world, and how did she build the life she lives today?

Don't worry; I have much more information in my brain that will be put on paper in the next few years.

I have already begun writing my second book called, *The Five Stages Of Leaving* which will be out soon. In this book I will give an unprecedented look of what it takes to go against everything I was taught to live a happy life.

To receive updates of the progress of this book visit my website at www.GrowingUpAmish.com Enter you name and email address and I will keep you updated. I promise to never sell, trade, or share your information with anyone.

ABOUT THE AUTHOR

TODAY LIFE IS VERY DIFFERENT for me. I live in a small community in northwestern Minnesota with my husband and two children. Currently I have a full time job to help my husband support our lifestyle. I really enjoy spending time with our children, camping, biking, and walking. Other hobbies I will engage in when possible is knitting and crocheting, sewing, gardening and canning, and volunteering my time to help out in our church and local community.

Although we live with all the modern conveniences that America has to offer today, I also implement as much of the simple lifestyle as possible. I always have plenty of canned goods stored away. Every summer at strawberry harvest time I will make enough jam for another year. I love preparing food for my family just as I did while growing up. The only difference today is that I only prepare food for four people instead of twelve. I had to learn to prepare small amounts of food.

My greatest passion is to share my experiences to help others. I have spoken to thousands of people of all ages. Many questions have come my way and I have had to do research to get some of the answers because it wasn't something that was talked about in my childhood home or community. For example: Someone asked me "What nationality are you?" I was not sure until I did some research and finally had a chance to talk to my father about it. Then I found out I is not German.....I am Dutch and Swiss. Most people would guess the Amish to be of German descent and some probably are but not in our family.

I have developed a home-study course and personal coaching program to assist people in using the tips and strategies that I implemented to overcome my obstacles. I asked myself this question many times: "Where do I belong and why am I here on earth?" and I am sure many still do. Because of my experiences

I now understand and these programs are designed to help you define this question.

I am also writing my next book where I will be talking about the transition years and what kind of mindset it took for me to go against every belief, understanding, and right thing I had ever known so I could live the lifestyle I had dreamed of.

All of this information is available from her website at

www.GrowingUpAmish.com

BONUSES

Sign Up Today
For Your Subscription To The One & Only Amish Reality TV

6 Months Free

A $97.00 Value

NOW THAT YOU HAVE READ the book; do you have more questions? No problem....there are two ways to get your questions answered directly from me.

- Join me on my next FREE teleseminar.

- Submit your question at http://www.growingupamish.com/askanna.htm and I will answer the question in video format via the internet or audio CD.

Mail in the coupon below or go to
http://www.growingupamish.com/amish-tv-signup.htm
to get started.

Yes Anna! Send me 6 months Amish Reality TV Shows **FREE**

Name: _____

Address: _____

Email: _____ Phone: _____

Credit Card Type: _____ Exp: _____

Credit Card #: _____

MAIL THIS COUPON TO:

GrowingUpAmish.com

100 Boardman Ave

New York Mills, MN 56567

*Shipping and Handling not included.

Printed in the United States
109599LV00001BA/1-45/A